John Johnson, Arthur Mazÿck

Historic Points of Interest in and around Charleston

John Johnson, Arthur Mazÿck

Historic Points of Interest in and around Charleston

ISBN/EAN: 9783337193614

Printed in Europe, USA, Canada, Australia, Japan

Cover: Foto ©Andreas Hilbeck / pixelio.de

More available books at **www.hansebooks.com**

Historic

Points of Interest

. . . In and Around . .

Charleston,

S. C.

**CONVENIENTLY ARRANGED FOR EASY REFERENCE
BY DATES, EVENTS AND PLACES.**

CONFEDERATE RE-UNION EDITION.

CHARLESTON, S. C.
1895.

Historic

Points of Interest

In and Around

Charleston, S. C.

CONVENIENTLY ARRANGED FOR EASY REFERENCE
BY DATES, EVENTS AND PLACES.

COPYRIGHT 1896.

CONFEDERATE RE-UNION EDITION.

CHARLESTON, S. C.
1896.

INDEX TO EVENTS.

INDEX TO EVENTS.

INDEX TO PLACES.

INDEX TO PLACES.

ARTISTS.

W. D. Clark, 265 King st.

BANKS.

American Savings Bank, 35 Broad Street. Capital $15,000. Surplus $14,000. W. M. Connor, President; T. M. McTureous, Cashier. Directors—W. M. Connor, B. A. Hagood, W. P. Sellers, T. G. Disher.

Bank of Charleston, N. B. A. Broad and State Sts Capital $300,000. Surplus, and undivided profits, $100,000 E. H. Pringle, President; M. W. Wilson, Cashier; Directors, E. H. Pringle, Geo. A. Wagener, A. S. Smith, J. M. Seignous, A. M. Lee.

Carolina Savings Bank, Broad and East Bay. Capital and resources $1,839,061.57. George W. Williams, President; George W. Williams, Jr., Vice-President; Henry P. Williams, Cashier.

Charleston under the Lords Proprietors.

Old Town on the West Bank of the Ashley.

The first permanent settlers in Carolina were English Emigrants sent out by the Lords Proprietors under the leadership of Col. William Sayle. They arrived in the year 1670 and established themselves on the West Bank of the Ashley River, a little above Wappoo Creek, and there laid out a town which they called *Charles Town.* Of this noth-thing now remains but a ditch or two, said to mark some of the old sites, and the name "Old Town Creek," character-izing the creek which formed one of the boundaries. The land covered by the town is now a farm owned by Mr. Edward T. Legare.

Oyster Point Town.

This settlement being soon found inconvenient, its in-habitants began to move across the river and downward to Oyster Point at the confluence of the Ashley and Cooper Rivers, and in 1672 Lots were laid out there. By the year 1677, they had a settlement large enough to need a name, and they called it *Oyster Point Town.*

New Charles-Town.

In 1680 the seat of government was removed to the new settlement which was then known as New Charlestown, and in the next two years the original settlement was practically abandoned, and the town took its name of Charles Town which it retained until its incorporation under its present designation in 1783.

The English Church—St. Philip's Parish.

When the new town was laid out the lot at the South-East Corner of what are now Broad and Meeting Streets—the present site of St. Michael's Church—was assigned to the English Church, and in 1681-2 a wooden building was there erected, the Parish being designated St. Philip's. In 1711, an Act was passed for building a new Church of brick, on the site of the present St. Philip's, East side of Church Street, between Queen and Cumberland Streets. It was opened for service in 1723, and was regarded as one of the finest churches in America. On February 15th, 1835, this beautiful old building, the most valuable, historically, in Charleston, perhaps in all the South, was completely de-

BANKS.

Enterprise Bank, 201 King street. Capital, $50,000 ; surplus, $5,000; J. J. Wescoat, Prest. ; W. G. Harvey, Jr., Cashier. Directors : J. J. Wescoat, N. A Hunt, Ed. Anderson, W. H. Welch, R. B. Lebby, A. S. Brown, T. S. Wilbur, W. Hartz, J. H. Jahnz.

Hibernia Savings Bank, 42 Broad Street. Capital $30,000 ; surplus $12,000 ; undivided profits $5,500. F. Q. O'Neill, President. J. J. O'Connell, Cashier ; J. E. Burke, Solicitor. Directors—B. O'Neill, T. R. McGahan, J. F. Redding, S. Fogarty, M. Revel, D. O'Brien, F. Q. O'Neill.

People's National Bank, 15 Broad Street. Capital $250,000; surplus $125,000 ; undivided profits $58,000. C. O. Witte, President , E. H. Sparkman, Cashier. Directors—C. O. Witte, Alva Gage, C. H. Drayton, A. B. Murray, A. F. C. Cramer. Joseph Thompson, W. B. Whaley, J. F. Redding, E. H. Sparkman, Samuel Lapham.

Security Savings Bank, 15 Broad Street. Capital $50,000. C. O. Witte, President ; E. H. Sparkman, Cashier. Directors— C. O. Witte, A. B. Murray, Joseph Thompson, J. N. Nathans, E. H. Sparkman, C. H. Drayton.

stroyed by fire. The present edifice was opened for worship 3rd May, 1838. Many interesting monuments of distinguished citizens may be seen in the church-yard, and near the centre of the Western cemetery rest the remains of Carolina's greatest son, John C. Calhoun.

The fine chime of bells belonging to this Church were cast into cannon during the late war.

The Independent Church—The Presbyterians:

In 1682 the Independents and the Presbyterians established a church. In an early Plan we find "The Independent Church" on the site on the East side of Meeting Street below Cumberland, now occupied by the Congregationalist Church. There was erected about 1790, a wooden building, known to the community as the "White Meeting House, and which probably gave the name to Meeting Street. This was replaced in 1804 by the "Circular Church," so called from its peculiar construction. This handsome building was destroyed by the great fire December, 1861, and the congregation worshipped in a small chapel erected in the grounds until the completion of the present church in 1890.

In the cemetery which runs back to that of St. Philip's are to be found the memorials of the founders of the Church and of many eminent citizens.

The Baptist Church,

West side Church street, above Water street. The organization of the Baptists in Charleston dates back to the year 1685. In 1699, lot No. 62, in the original plan of Charles-Town, was given by William Elliott to the congregation, and a church building erected on it. This was replaced by the present building of the First Baptist Church, described by Mills in his Statistics of So. Ca., (1826) as exhibiting "the best specimen of correct taste in architecture of the modern buildings in this city."

Representing the original organization of the Baptists, its cemetery and the tablets on its walls exhibit the memorials of the founders of that denomination in Carolina.

The Huguenots, French Protestant Church,

South East corner Church and Queen Streets. Among the first settlers of the Province, there were French Protestants, and in 1680 some others arrived. But the principal and largest immigration of Huguenots was in the year immediately following the Revocation of the Edict of Nantes, (1685).

J. R. JOHNSON & SON,

✦ Hatters. ✦

MEN'S FURNISHERS,
UMBRELLA MANUFACTURERS,

253 KING ST., opp. Hasell.

BANKS.

South Carolina Loan and Trust Company, 17 Broad Street. Authorized Capital $500,000 ; paid up $250,000. E. H. Frost, President ; F. A. Mitchell, Cashier. Directors—G. L. Buist, A. Canale, E. H. Frost, S. R. Marshall, William L. Webb, H. W. Frost, A. Gastaver.

State Savings Bank, 49 Broad street. Capital and Resources, $150,000 ; Isaac S. Cohen, Prest ; Lee Loeb, Vice-Prest.; R. B. Gilchrist, Cashier. Directors : Jno B. Reeves, Lee Loeb, E. S. Burnham, I. V. Bardin, Isaac S.Cohen.

BAKERS.

F. Heinz & Son,   King Street.
O. G. Marjenhoff, 147, 149 and 151 Church Street.

BAKERS' SUPPLIES.

O. G. Marjenhoff, 147, 149, 151 Church Street.

BICYCLE DEALERS.

Cameron & Barkley Co., 160, 164 Meeting Street (Imperial, Windsor and Czar.)
Charleston Cycle Co, 310 King Street. (Columbias.)
Muckenfuss & Harvey, King Street, Y. M. C. A. Building. Helical Premier, Erie and others.)
A. S. Thomas, 211, 213 King Street. (Sterling.)
Valk & Murdock Iron Works, 12, 20 Hasell Street. (Warwick Perfection Cushion Frame.)

10

Within a very few years a church was erected on the site occupied by the present edifice. Twice their buildings were destroyed by fire and the congregation scattered. In 1843 the present small, but very pretty building was erected.

This has a peculiar interest from its historic associations, and the handsome tablets on its wall commemorating the principal founders.

This congregation is the only one in America that adheres to the original liturgy of the French Protestant Church—the services were for upwards of a hundred and fifty years conducted in French, but about the time of the re-opening of the Church, a translation was made.

Topography in 1704.

A Plan of Charles-Town, as laid out by John Culpepper in 1680, with the buildings and fortifications, in 1704, by Edward Crisp, gives us a curious view of the topography of the city in its very early days.

The boundaries then were. on the north, a creek running where the market now stands; on the east Cooper River, the bank of which was a good deal further in than now, the water covering the space now occupied by the offices, warehouses, &c., east of East Bay street; on the south, a creek known as Vander Horst's Creek, and covering what is now Water Street, while the western boundary was a little beyond Meeting Street. The intersection of Broad and Church Streets, was about the central point of the town.

On the east side of Bay Street, directly opposite Broad, was the Court of Guards or Garrison.

At or near the western limit, where the City Hall now stands, was the Public Market Opposite was the English Church. (St. Philip's,) on the site of the present St. Michael's.

The site of the Court House was a large pond, probably artificial, the earth having been dug out to erect defences.

The French Church, the Independent, and the Baptist, were on the sites now occupied by them respectively.

There was a Quaker Meeting House, but that was outside of the limits of the town, on a lot on the east side of King street a short distance below Queen, where some grave stones may still be seen.

Tradd's house stood on the Northwest corner of Tradd and East Bay Streets. This was the birth place of Robert Tradd, said to have been the first child born in the town.

Langrave Thomas Smith's house, was on the southwest corner of East Bay and Longitude Lane. On the lot in rear of this, it is believed that the first rice raised in Carolina was planted about the year 1693.

11

BLANK BOOK MANUFACTURERS.

Walker, Evans & Cogswell Co., 3 and 5 Broad and 117 East Bay Streets.

BOOKSELLERS & STATIONERS.

B. Doscher, 242 Meeting st.
Isaac Hammond, 10 Broad st.
C. L. Legerton, 282 King st.
A. W. Riecke, 311 King st.
Walker, Evans & Cogswell Co., 3 & 5 Broad and 117 E. Bay.

BOOTS & SHOES—(Retail.)

T. M. Bristol & Son, 236 King st.
Jas. D. Nelson, 320 King st.

BOOTS & SHOES—(Wholesale)

Brown-Evans Co., 226 Meeting st.

12

The town consisted in all of eight streets and one alley, viz : Tradd, Elliott, Broad and Queen, (or Dock St., as it was first called,) running east and west, and Bay Union, (now State,) Church and Meeting Streets running North and South.

Bastions at the all salient points connected by earth works defended the inhabitants from foreign enemies and the neighboring Indians, and practically made Charles-Town a walled city.

The Revolution of 1719—Charles Town under the King.

The Province of Carolina

was up to this time under the exclusive government of the Lords Proprietors, administered by a Governor and Council, appointed by and representing them, according to the laws laid down in the famous fundamental Constitutions. or rather according to sets of " Instructions " issued by the Proprietors, as it was found impossible to put the Constitutions into practical effect.

Discontent of the people with this form of government culminated. in 1719, in a successful effort by which the Proprietary Governor, Robert Johnson, was deposed, and James Moore was installed by the people as their Governor, subject to the direct authority of the British Crown. Ten years later the Proprietors formally surrendered their charter, and at the same time the Province was divided into North and South Carolina.

South Carolina became then a Royal Province, and a favorite one, and Charles Town grew and flourished, ranking with the first cities of America.

To this period belongs the foundation of many religious, charitable and educational institutions, a large proportion of which exist to the present day.

1729—St. Andrew's Society,

founded 1729, by Scotchmen, for charitable purposes, is the oldest Society in Charleston. The Society owned a fine hall in Broad street, (the place of meeting of the Secession Convention) which was destroyed by the fire of 1861. The lot on which it stood is owned by Captain F. W. Wagener, and is still vacant.

BROKERS—BONDS & STOCK.

E. M. Moreland, 29 Broad st.

BUILDERS' MATERIALS & SUPPLIES.

South-Eastern Lime and Cement Co., 276, 278 East Bay.

CANDY MANUFACTURERS

F. Heinz & Son, 387-241 King st.
O. G. Marjenhoff, 147, 149, 151 Church st.

CARPET DEALERS.

Mutual Carpet Co., 247 King st.

CARRIAGE MAKERS.

E. W. Benedikt, Wentworth and Meeting sts.

CIGARS AND TOBACCOS.—(Retail.)

Gotjen, Anton & Co., King and Market sts.
A. W. Riecke, 311 King Street.

CIGARS AND TOBACCOS.—(Wholesale.)

O. G. Marjenhoff, 147, 149, 151 Church Street.

14

1736—The South Carolina Society

was founded by Huguenots, and was known originally as the Two-Bit Club, from the small sum(two bits or four half pence) contributed at every meeting by each member, for the relief of the indigent among them. It was incorporated in 1751. Larger subscriptions and many donations and bequests increased the funds of the Society rapidly, and it became one of the wealthiest in the community. Besides pensioning the widows and orphans of its members, a free school was established by the Society, which for some years previous to the establishment of a free school system by the city, gave education of a large number of children. For the purposes of this school and the general meetings of the Society, the hall on the east side of Meeting street, above Tradd, was built. On the front of the colonade, which extends over the side walk, the seal of the Society is represented, a hand, holding an olive branch with the legend " *Posteritati.*"

2d Presbyterian(Scotch)Church. S.W. cor. Meeting & Tradd.

In the year 1731 the strict Presbyterians among the congregation of the Independent Church left it and established a Church for themselves after the form of the Church of Scotland. They were incorporated in 1784. They erected a church on the lot at the corner of Meeting and Tradd Streets, which was replaced by the present massive structure. The interior of this Church was remodeled after the earthquake of 1886, and the contrast between the stern, almost rugged exterior, and the highly finished, comfortable interior is striking. In the Church and its adjoining cemetery may be seen the monuments of its founders and the names of some of the best known families of the community.

Charleston Library Building, N. W. cor. Broad & Church Sts.

The Charleston Library Society was organized in 1748, being the third Library established in America. It was chartered in 1754. The books were at first kept at the residence of the Librarian, then in the third story of the State House, (now the Court House.) In 1778, the collection of books, already very valuable, was destroyed by fire. The Library now numbers only some 20,000 volumes, but among these are an unusual number of rare and valuable works.

In 1835 the present building, erected for and occupied by the South Carolina Bank, was purchased by the Society.

CLOTHING.—(Wholesale.)

Brown-Evans Co., 226 Meeting Street.
T. A. Wilbur & Son, 211 Meeting Street.

CLOTHING.—(Retail.)

Bentschner & Visanska, 252 King Street.
J. L. David & Bro., 278, 281 King Street.

CONFECTIONERY.

Gotjen, Anton & Co., King and Market Streets.
F. Heins & Son, 387-241 King Street.

CROCKERY AND GLASSWARE.

Wm. L. Webb, 215 Meeting Street.

DENTIST.

Dr. J. A Miles, 69 Hasell st.

DRY GOODS AND NOTIONS.—(Retail.)

J. R. Read & Co., 249 King Street.
The Bon Marche, 259 King Street.

DRY GOODS AND NOTIONS.—(Wholesale.)

T. R. McGahan & Co., 228 Meeting Street.
T. A. Wilbur & Son, 211 Meeting Street.

Charleston during the Revolutionary War

The Revolution of 1776.

Carolina was a favorite province with the British Government, and Charles-Town, its chief city, flourished under the Royal rule, but the spirit of resistance to encroachments on their liberties, and a warm sympathy with the other American Colonies brought her people early into the Revolutionary struggle. Nowhere was the Stamp Act more vigorously opposed, and the odious Tea tax was resisted in Charles-Town in a manner, not so dramatic as in Boston, but quite as effectual, the consignees of the cargoes themselves refusing to receive the tea and destroying such as was landed openly and of their own will.

The first blood shed in the war was in the famous battle of Fort Moultrie, June 28th, 1776, when the little palmetto fort on Sullivan's Island, where the present fort stands, successfully repulsed a powerful British fleet.

Charles-Town had her full share of the horrors of war. On the 12th of May, 1780, after a siege of four months and a heavy bombardment, the city was surrendered to the British and held under military rule until evacuated by them December 14th, 1782.

There are venerable buildings and interesting relics still to be seen connected with this period of the city's history.

St. Michael's Church, s. e. cor. Meeting and Broad Sts.

An Act of Assembly in 1751, divided Charles-Town into two Parishes, St. Philip's and St. Michael's, that south of Broad Street to be called St. Michael's, and a parish church to be built "on or near the place where the old church of St. Philip stood." The church was opened for worship February 1st, 1761. The bells and clock were brought from England in 1764 and the organ in 1768.

At the evacuation of Charles-Town by the British in 1782, Major Traille, of the Royal Artillery, took possession of the bells as a military perquisite and shipped them to England; a Mr. Ryhiner purchased them in London and sent them back in 1783. During the late war they were sent to Columbia, S. C., for safety and when Gen. Sherman burned that city in 1865, two were stolen and the rest so injured as to be useless. In 1866 they were again shipped to England, recast by the successors of the firm which had originally made them from the same patterns and again returned to Charleston and replaced in the belfry on 21st March, 1867.

DRUGS.

G. W. Aimar & Co., King & Vanderhorst sts.
Palmetto Pharmacy, 286–288 King Street.

FLAGS AND BADGES.

C. L. Legerton, 282 King Street.

FRUITS.—(Wholesale.)

C. Bart & Co., 77, 79, 81 Market Street.
H. Bayer & Son, 134 Meeting Street.

FURNITURE.

W. P. Seilers, 196, 198 King Street.
A. S. Thomas, 211, 213 King Street.

GASOLINE, GASOLINE STOVES AND ALUMINUM WARE.

Adam Roessler, 250 Meeting Street.

GROCERIES—(Retail.)

Gotjen, Anton & Co., corner King and Market Sts.

18

St. Michael's is the most interesting monument of Colonial days to be found in Charleston.

The Old Post Office—Formerly the "Exchange"

In 1767 an Act was passed by the General Assembly for the building of an "Exchange and Custom House and New Watch House for the service of the Government," and the commissioners appointed under this Act gave the contract for the work to Messrs. Peter and John Horlbeck, one of whose descendants now possesses the original contract.

The work was completed in 1771, and the building used as an Exchange for the merchants of the city and for a Custom House.

During the occupation of Charleston by the British, 1780–81, it was taken for the "Provost" of the commandant and the cellars were used as a prison for the citizens arrested by the military authorities. In one of these cellars Col. Isaac Hayne was confined and thence led to execution.

Gen. Washington appeared before the citizens of Charleston on the steps of this building on his visit to the city in 1791, and the grand concert and ball given in his honor were held here. The building was sold to the United States Government in 1818, for a Postoffice and has been so used until the completion of the new Government building. It is proposed again to obtain it for the city for its original purpose of an Exchange for merchants.

Pringle House, w. side of King St., Second Above Lamboll.

This is one of the oldest houses in Charleston, and is probably the best preserved and most elegant specimen of Colonial architecture. It was built by Miles Brewton about 1765. He, with his whole family, was lost at sea and the house passed to his three sisters, one of whom, Mrs. Rebecca Motte, famous in Revolutionary story, was living in it at the time of the occupation of the city by the British—1781-2. The house was taken by Sir Henry Clinton as headquarters, and after him by Lord Rawdon.

When the United States forces occupied Charleston, 1865, this house was again selected as the headquarters of the commanding general.

The William Washington House.

The large wooden house at the northwest corner of South Battery and Church Street, now the residence of Mr. R. B. Dowie, belongs to the Colonial period, and was the property of Colonel William Washington, of Revolutionary fame. It was here that Mrs. Washington, in 1827, presented her

HARDWARE.

Cameron & Barkley Co., 160-164 Meeting Street.
Marshall, Wescoat & Co., 207 Meeting Street.

HATS AND CAPS.—(Retail.)

Bentschner & Visanska, 252 King Street.
J. L. David & Bro., 279, 281 King Street.
J. R. Johnson & Son, 253 King Street, opposite Hasell.

HOTELS.

St. Charles, Meeting and Hasell.

HOUSE FURNISHING GOODS.

R. J. Morris, 130 King St.
Mutual Carpet Company, 247 King St.
Shepherd Supply Company, 232 Meeting St.
A. S. Thomas, 211, 213 King St.

husband's battle flag—the famous Eutaw flag—to the Washington Light Infantry.

Judge Heyward's House, where Washington was Entertained

The house No. 87 Church Street, east side, above Tradd, now occupied by Mr. H. W. Fuseler as a residence and bakery, is a particularly interesting memorial of the visit of General Washington to Charleston in May, 1791. Mr. Charles Fraser, in his Reminiscences, says: "I remember "that the place prepared for his accommodation was that "large three-story, double house in Church Street, north of "Tradd, then owned by Judge Heyward and said to be "superbly furnished for the occasion. He remained here "but one week, but it was a week of continued rejoicing "and festivity.

The Old Magazine, Cumberland Street.

A curious relic of Continental days is a small octagonal brick building with four gables and tile-covered roof standing ruinous in an obscure lot in Cumberland street. This was a powder magazine. As early as 1770 an Act was passed directing the disuse of it, but the war coming on powder was stored there until during the siege of the city by the British (1780) a shell fell and exploded within a few feet of it. It was then abandoned and became private property. It has by some chance escaped entire demolition and ought now to be owned by the city and preserved as a memento of the olden times.

1766-1770—The Statue of Wm. Pitt in Washington Square

is a peculiarly interesting Revolutionary relic. Its history is briefly but clearly given on the two panels of its base.

After the Revolution.

Charleston Incorporated.

An Act of the Legislature, August 13, 1783, incorporated the "City Council of Charleston." The "Church Wardens of the Parish of St. Philip and St. Michael," were directed to conduct an election for Wardens—one for each of the thirteen wards—and these Wardens were afterwards to hold an election for Intendant.

Richard Hutson was the first Intendant thus chosen.

The city grew and prospered; revived the works begun

ICE—(Wholesale)

H. Bayer & Son, 184 Meeting St,
Charleston Ice Manufacturing Co., Anson & Market Sts.

ICE FACTORIES.

Charleston Ice Manufacturing Co., Anson & Market Sts.

ICE CREAM.

F. Heinz & Son, 387-241 King St.

INSURANCE.

C. T. Lowndes & Co., 14 Broad Street, General Agents Liverpool & London & Globe.

before the war and undertook new and more extended ones.

A few may be noted here :--

The Court House, N. W. Corner Broad and Meeting Streets.

In the early topography of Charles Town it was noted that this site was occupied by a pond. This was filled up and the State House erected on the spot. After that was burned in 1788 and the Legislature had removed its sittings to Columbia the present building was erected for the County (or District as it was then) Court House. The exterior has remained unchanged except by the shifting of the main entrance, but the interior has been several times remodelled.

1801-1802—City Hall N. E. Cor. Broad and Meeting Streets.

The square on which this building stands was in Colonial times the Town market-place. In 1801-2 the building was erected by the United States Bank. After the expiration of the charter of the Bank the City, in 1818, purchased it for a City Hall. The very handsome marble pillars and facings of the exterior were imported from Italy by a gentleman of Philadelphia for his private residence.

The interior, which has more than once been remodeled, is now most admirably arranged to contain the Council Chamber and all the city offices. In the Council Chamber and Mayor's office adjoining are a remarkably interesting collection of portraits and busts.

The Charleston Orphan House, Calhoun Street.

This noble charity has enlisted the sympathy and received the aid of the citizens of Charleston more liberally and continuously than any other institution within its limits.

The Act of incorporation imposed upon the city the duty of providing for the poor and maintaining and educating poor orphan children. These duties, it may be observed, had in Colonial times devolved upon the Parish authorities, that is, the vestries of the Church of England establishment, St. Philip's and St. Michael's.

In 1792 the City Council passed an Ordinance for the erection of an Orphan House and appropriated the lands now occupied for that purpose.

On 12th November, 1792, the corner-stone of the building was laid, and two years later the Institution was opened, and one hundred and fifteen orphan children received into it. In 1855 the present much enlarged and beautiful building was completed.

IRON WORKS.

Charleston Iron Works, Pritchard, near East Bay.
Valk & Murdoch Iron Works, 12-20 Hasell St.

JEWELRY AND SILVERWARE.

James Allan & Co., 285 King St.
S. Thomas & Bro., 257 King St.

MACHINERY.

Cameron & Barkley Company, 160-164 Meeting St.

MARBLE AND GRANITE WORKS.

Thomas H. Reynolds, 122-128 King St.

The Central Market, Meeting Street,

was established between 1788 and 1804. It extends from Meeting to East Bay Street. The Market Hall, fronting Meeting Street, is an imposing structure, its cornices appropriately adorned with bulls' heads.

The Unitarian Church, east-side of Archdale St.,

Was erected just before the Revolutionary War for a branch of the Congregationalist Church. The congregation adopted the Unitarian Doctrine under the pastorate of the Rev. Anthony Foster about 1817. The present building was erected on the old foundations and walls and dedicated in 1854. It is a peculiarly beautiful piece of architecture in what is known as the "Perpendicular" style of the Gothic. Recently a large and perfectly appointed Sunday-School and Pastor's residence has been erected next, south of the Church, through the munificence of a member of the congregation.

St. John's Lutheran Church, cor. Archdale & Clifford Sts.

This represents the oldest German Congregation in the city. They built a church as early as 1759, and were incorporated in 1783. The present building was completed and dedicated January 8, 1818.

This church is inseparably connected with the memory of the venerable Dr. John Bachman for sixty years its pastor, distinguished not only for his piety and good works, but also for his high attainments and as the friend and co-laborator of Audubon. The interior of the Church has been quite recently remodeled and greatly beautified.

Bethel Methodist Epis'l Church, W. side Pitt, cor. Calhoun.

The Methodist Church was organized in America in 1784, and at once took root in Charleston. A wooden building was erected on the site above mentioned in 1795, and that building, now removed to an adjacent lot in the rear, is used by a colored congregation. The present Church was dedicated in 1853, and is a simple but finely proportioned structure.

St. Mary's Church—Roman Catholic—Hasell Street

Was the first Roman Catholic Church in South Carolina, and on its walls and its Cemetery may be seen the memorials of the early members of that faith in the city. The site has been in occupation since 1789, the present is the third building erected there, and was built about 1840. It

MATTINGS AND OILCLOTH.

Mutual Carpet Company, 247 King St.

MEN'S FURNISHINGS.

Bentschner & Visanska, 252 King St.
J. L. David & Bro., 279, 281 King St.
J. R. Johnson & Son, 253 King St., opposite Hasell.

NEWS DEPOTS.

B. Doscher, 242 Meeting St.
C. L. Legerton, 282 King St.
A. W. Riecke, 311 King St.

has recently been renovated and improved, and a new and very fine organ provided.

Roman Catholic Cathedral, St. Finbar's, Broad Street.

Corner-stone laid in 1852 and the Church dedicated 1854. It was the handsomest church building in Charleston, was destroyed in the great fire, December, 1861, since which time the services have been conducted in the Cathedral Chapel on Queen Street.

In 1881 a large bequest was made by a member of the congregation and the building now in process of erection was begun on the same design as the former one.

The Hebrew Synagogue, Hasell Street.

A Hebrew congregation existed in Charleston in 1750. In 1795 they purchased the site of their present Synagogue. It is a very handsome building, not situated so as to show to advantage, but well worthy of examination. Its membership is large and the congregation well sustained.

College of Charleston, George, Green, St. Philip & College.

The College was chartered in 1785 and established in a brick building on the line of College Street used by the British during the Revolution as barracks, and after that by the Rev. Robert Smith, (afterwards first Bishop of South Carolina) as a school-house. The first Commencement was in 1794. In 1828 a new building was erected to which was added subsequently, extensive wings. The College has been the "*Alma Mater*" of many of the most distinguished citizens of the State. It is well equipped and possesses a remarkably fine Museum of Natural History— as well as an excellent Library, chiefly of classical literature.

The High School, n. w. cor. Meeting and George Sts.,

Is a City Institution for classical education. It has long filled a useful place, and in recent years there being less competition from private schools, has rapidly advanced in its standards and the number of scholars. In 1880, the present building, formerly the residence of Hon. Mitchell King, was purchased and the school removed from its former smaller quarters in Society Street. Recent additions have been made in the building and all the equipments of a first-rate modern school have been supplied.

27

OFFICE FURNITURE AND SUPPLIES.

Walker, Evans & Cogswell Company, 3 & 5 Broad and 117 East Bay Sts.

OILS.

Cameron & Barkley Co., 160-164 Meeting St.

OIL GAS STOVES.

R. J. Morris, 130 King St.

PAINTS, OILS AND GLASS.

Wm. M. Bird & Co, 205 East Bay.
Jas. Ackerman & Co., 177 King st.

Medical College of the State of South Carolina, Queen St.

was chartered in 1852, succeeding a School of Medicine organized in 1822, under the auspices of the Medical Society of South Carolina. It has always had the support of the leading members of the medical profession in the city and numbers among its graduates men of national reputation. The College is now in active operation, graduating large classes every year—has a full and able corps of Professors, keeps fully abreast of the times, but adheres to the three years' course and a rigid standard of excellence to obtain its diploma.

The Citadel—Marion Square.

The idea of a State Military School to take the place of the company of soldiers kept as a magazine guard at the Citadel in Charleston and the Arsenal in Columbia, originated with Governor John P. Richardson in 1841, and by 1843 the schools were established, separately at first, but soon united under one control. The Academy soon rose to a high place among the educational institutions of the South, and its graduates have occupied the most conspicuous places in military and civil life. The Battery which fired on the "Star of the West," when she attempted to relieve Fort Sumter in 1861, was manned by the Citadel Cadets. The Cadets served on all occasions of emergency in and around Charleston during the war, and in December, 1864 went into active service, and so continued until the close of hostilities. The Academy buildings were used as barracks by the Federal troops while they garrisoned the city, and during their occupation the west wing was burned. In 1882, through the exertions of some of its graduates the Academy was re-opened here, and has since had a flourishing existence. Its standard of education is high, and in military drill and discipline it is recognized in the reports of the United States inspecting officers as being in the first rank of military schools in the country.

On Marion Square may be seen a specimen of the old "Tapia," or more commonly called "Tabby" work, part of the old Revolutionary lines of defence.

PAINTERS AND PAPER HANGERS.

Jas. Ackerman, 177 King st.

PANTS, SHIRTS & UNDERWEAR MANUFACTURERS.

Phillips & Meyers, 233 Meeting st. (Pants a specialty.)

PHOTOGRAPHERS.

Dowling, the veteran in Photography, 305 King st.
W. D. Clark, 265 King st.
W. B. Austin, Vandyke Studio, 310 King st.

PICTURES AND PICTURE FRAMES.

C. L. Legerton, 282 King st.

3

CHARLESTON

During the Period of the Confederacy.

Dec. 20, 1860—The **Ordinance** of Secession,

passed by the Convention of the State of South Carolina, at St. Andrew's Hall, No. 118 Broad St., was ratified that evening at the So. Ca. Institute Hall, No. 134 Meeting St. Both buildings were destroyed in the great fire of December 1861.

Dec. 26. 1860—**Fort Moultrie Evacuated,**

and Fort Sumter occupied by Maj. Anderson, commanding U. S. troops.

Dec. 27-30, 1860—**U. S. Forts, Arsenal, and Property Seized**

Jan. 9, 1861—**The first gun of the War fired**

at the transport steamer "Star of the West," attempting to reinforce Fort Sumter, but stopped by the guns of the Morris Island battery, manned by Cadets of the S. C. Military Academy. Although struck, the steamer was not injured but returned to New York without communicating with Fort Sumter. Maj. Anderson refrained from returning the fire, but demanded an explanation of the Governor of the State.

April 12-14, 1861—**Fort Sumter bombarded.**

Soon after the organization of the Southern Confederacy, General Beauregard was ordered to conduct military operations against Fort Sumter. When it became known that a second attempt to relieve the garrison would be made by the Federal government, preparations for attack were hastened ; and, when completed, the surrender of the Fort was demanded by the Confederates. The demand being refused, the batteries from Sullivan's, Morris' and James Islands, were opened according to notice, before daylight on the 12th of April. Firing from these, was maintained for thirty-three hours, and replied to by the Fort. At length, on the second day, the quarters having been set on fire by hot shot, and the smoke becoming intolerable, the fort was surrendered. The garrison, after saluting their flag, were conveyed by the Confederates, April 14th, to the three gunboats and a troop-ship, which had come to their aid, but

PLUMBERS, GAS AND STEAM FITTERS.

R. J. Morris, 130 King st.

PRINTERS, BINDERS AND LITHOGRAPHERS.

Walker, Evans & Cogswell Co., 3 and 5 Broad and 117 East Bay sts.

RESTAURANTS.

F. Heinz & Son, 387, 241 King st.

had remained idle spectators of the bombardment. Embarking on these, the garrison were taken to New York. But few casualties had occurred on either side. The use of iron-plating for the protection of batteries, and of a rifled cannon imported from England, marked the introduction of these two elements by the Confederates into American warfare.

May 11th, 1861—The Blockade of Charleston Harbor,

begun by the steam-frigate Niagara, was maintained subsequently by a large squadron of armored vessels and wooden gun-boats.

June 16th, 1862—Battle of Secessionville,

James Island, five miles from Charleston. Union troops assault the earthworks with a full division and are repulsed with a loss of nearly seven hundred men. The Confederates, numbering 750 in the works, lost but two hundred and four. The Union troops evacuated James Island early in the next month.

Jan. 30th, 1863—Capture of the U. S. Gunboat Isaac Smith

The Federal gunboat, Isaac Smith, (eleven guns) was captured in Stono River, six miles from the city, by a combination of light-artillery and infantry in ambuscade on James and John's Islands; prisoners were taken, to the number of 11 officers and 108 men, among whom were 24 casualties.

Jan. 31st, 1863—Attack by Confederate Gunboats.

The two Confederate armored gun-boats, Palmetto State and Chicora, newly completed in Charleston, attacked the blockading squadron before daylight, driving the vessels off, four or five miles outside the bar. Two of the blockaders were temporarily disabled and surrendered, but managed to escape, with forty-seven casualties on board. This attack came near to being a great success. The Confederate boats were unhurt, but being very slow were unable to secure the fruits of victory.

February 13th, 1863—Running the Blockade.

Three steamers with cotton run the blockade, and one enters from Nassau, N. Providence, this night.

March 28th—U. S. Forces occupy Stono Inlet and Islands.

Occupation of Cole's and Folly Islands and Stono Entrance by U. S. forces under General Hunter.

Charleston Ice Mfg. Co.
Pure Crystal
ICE
PACKED ICE FOR COUNTRY TRADE A SPECIALTY.
N. E. Cor. Market and Church Sts.

RUBBER STAMPS AND SUPPLIES

Walker, Evans & Cogswell Co., 3 and 5 Broad and 117 East Bay sts.

SADDLERY AND HARNESS.

F. H. Warren, 223 Meeting st.

SHADES AND DRAPERIES.

Mutual Carpet Co., 247 King st.

Apr. 7th, 1863—The Repulse of the Iron-Clad Squadron.

Rear Admiral DuPont, commanding an iron-clad squadron of eight monitors and the steam frigate New Ironsides, attacked Fort Sumter, drawing the fire of the Sullivan's Island batteries also. In an action of two hours and thirty minutes, five out of the nine vessels were disabled, and one of these, the Keokuk, sank off Morris Island next morning. The fort with a garrison of 550 men, commanded by Col. Rhett, First S. C. Artillery, was seriously damaged in two or three places, but made ready to renew the fight next day. The casualties on both sides were slight. Union, 23; Confederate, 6. This memorable repulse of the armored vessels proved the readiness of the South, in at least one place, to meet the strongest effort of the United States Navy. In point of both armament and power of resistance, it was the most formidable naval attack made up to that time, in this, or any other country. The squadron carried a total of thirty-two guns, apportioned as follows :—twenty-two of eleven inches, smooth bore, seven of fifteen inches, (s. b.) and three Parrot rifle cannon of eight inches calibre. The Confederates had many guns of no value against armored vessels, and none heavier than the smooth-bore ten-inch Columbiads. An important place in the action was filled by the rope-obstruction across the channel, between Fort Sumter and Sullivan's Island. This, buoyed with beer-kegs for floats, was supposed to be a line of torpedoes, and effectually stopped the advance of the entire squadron into the inner harbor. The attack was not renewed, the Rear Admiral deciding against so doing, and being removed on that account from command of the squadron. Three or four of the armored vessels were under repair for several weeks after the action. Mr. Swinton, the war correspondent of the North, wrote at the time :—"As one of the leading actions of the war, the battle of Charleston Harbor passes into history and takes its place there. As a contribution to the world's experience in the art of iron-clad warfare, it passes into science and opens an epoch there." The land-forces, under General Hunter, took no part in the movement, but remained on Folly Island, until after the naval action.

April 9, 1863—Federal Signals Read by the Confederates.

The key having been discovered, signals made between the fleet and the land forces of the United States were read by the defenders of Charleston from this date onward. This advantage was not always available, but did serve a purpose occasionally.

SOUVENIR SPOONS.

Jas. Allen & Co., 285 King st.

STOVES AND TINWARE.

R. J. Morris, 130 King st.
Shepherd Supply Co., 232 Meeting st.

TAILORS.

John Rugheimer, 169 King st.

TIN PLATES AND SHEET METALS.

Shepherd Supply Co., 232 Meeting st.

April-May, 1836—An Imperfect Blockade of Charleston.

By official returns of the Collector it appears that during these two months 15 vessels entered, 21 cleared the port, while 10,003 bales of cotton were exported The total receipts of customs were $138,520. The blockade squadron was large and vigilant, but was continually eluded by small, swift steamers, (Clyde-built)running between Charleston and Nassau, a port in the Bahama Islands, In return for cotton the vessels brought back arms, manufactured goods and supplies for public and private benefit.

April-May, 1863—Recovery of the Guns of the "Keokuk."

This bold and brilliant achievement by the Confederates occupied about three weeks of limited night-work. It was conducted with great perils and difficulties, but with distinguished enterprise and perseverance, enabling Charleston to become possessed of two of the proudest and most formidable trophies of the war, heavy guns, which were immediately put to use in the defense of the harbor.

June-July 10th, 1863.—Descent on Morris Island.

The Confederates, under Gen. Beauregard, fortified this island, being about four miles long, with Battery Gregg at its northern end, Cumming's Point, and Battery or Fort Wagner three-fourths of a mile farther south. They were strong works, heavily armed, particularly Fort Wagner, which was large and formidable, by reason of its approaches, bomb-proof construction and armament. Both these works were within range of Fort Sumter's supporting fire. At the southern end of the island were some detached works, each carrying one gun or mortar, placed to dispute a landing from Light-house Inlet. Between the 7th April and 10th July, the Confederate forces had been reduced one-half against General Beauregard's earnest protests. Only 927 men, artillery and infantry, were thus available for the defense of Morris Island, when it was attacked July 10th with heavy bombardment from Folly Island, across the narrow inlet, and from monitors of the iron-clad squadron, with more than four times the number of guns and troops.

This bombardment of the southern end of Morris Island was followed by a landing of 2,000 Federal troops coming in barges by the inlet, and carrying every thing before them. The Confederates retired after four hours fighting, and were covered by Fort Wagner. The losses were, Confederate, 294. Federal, 106. The garrison of Fort Wagner was reinforced that night.

TIN, COPPER AND SHEET IRON WORKERS.

R. J. Morris, 130 King st.

TOBACCO BARN FLUES.

Shepherd Supply Co., 232 Meeting st.

TRAVELLING BAGS.

Charleston Trunk and Bag Emporium, 319 King Street.
T. M. Bristol & Son, 236 King st.

July 11-18, 1863—Two Assaults on Fort Wagner.

The first assault was made at early dawn, on the 11th, by a column of Federal troops. They were repulsed with a loss of 330. The Confederates had only twelve casualties.

On the morning of the 16th, a demonstration with troops and a naval support was made by the Federals, on James Island, by the way of Stono River. It was met by the Confederates, with loss on their part of 18, and on the Federal part of 50. The Union troops left the island that night.

Gen. Gillmore commanding the Union forces on land, with Rear Admiral Dahlgren co-operating by water, had occupied the larger part of Morris Island since the 10th. Having failed in one assault of Fort Wagner, he resolved to try another, after heavy bombardments of siege batteries and armored vessels. On the 18th, after a land and naval bombardment of uncommon severity, lasting eleven hours, the second assault with heavy forces was made at close of day, Gen'l. Taliaferro was in command of the Confederates in Fort Wagner, about 1,000 men. After a fierce struggle of nearly three hours, the Union troops were repulsed with heavy loss—reported by them at not less than 1,500. The Confederates lost 174.

The Union commander now determined to change his plan in two leading particulars. Fort Wagner was to be besieged with regular approaches, and Fort Sumter was to be demolished from ground already in his possession, at a distance of about 4,000 yards.

Aug. 4. 1863—Construction of the Marsh Battery.

by the Federals, between Morris and James Islands. Here the 200 pounder rifle, called by them "The Swamp Angel," was mounted, and opened fire on Charleston, 7,000 yards distant, August 21, 1863, bursting at the 36th round. This battery took no further part in the shelling of the city.

Aug. 17–Sep. 2, 1863—Fort Sumter demolished and silenced.

The rifled-cannon brought by Gen. Gillmore, were capable of unprecedented range, accuracy and destructive power. Fort Sumter was prepared for them by Gen. Beauregard, with such skill of foresight and contrivance as to entirely disappoint all hope of surrender. He had the fort armament reduced to a mimimum, casemates and rooms exposed to breaching filled-in with sand and wet compressed cotton-bales, and a new wharf built on the side of the city, protected by the fort itself.

But, when the breaching fire from eighteen rifle-cannon— 100, 200, and 300 pounders, began to be poured upon the de-

Dr. J. A. Miles,

DENTIST,

Established
1881.

69 HASELL ST.,
CHARLESTON, S. C.

TRUNKS.

Charleston Trunk and Bag Emporium, 319 King Street. (Repairing a Specialty.)
A. S. Thomas, 211, 213 King Street.
Jas. D. Nelson, 320 King Street.
T. M. Bristol & Son, 236 King Street.

TYPEWRITERS.

Walker, Evans & Cogswell Co., 3 and 5 Broad and 117 East Bay Streets. (Smith Premier.)

TYPEWRITER REPAIRING.

Walker, Evans & Cogswell Co., 3 and 5 Broad and 117 East Bay Streets.

voted fort, it became evident that its ruin, as a first-class fortification of its period, was assured. At the end of six-teen days, all-day firing, combined with two night attacks by the armored squadron, the fort was silenced, as well as demolished. But it was habitable, and the surrender was not considered for a moment by the Confederate General. It had received nearly 7,000 shot and shell, and its casualties had been two killed and 50 wounded. Its first great bom-bardment lasted thus sixteen days.

Sept. 4-6 1863—Morris Island Evacuated.

Col. Alfred Rhett, commanding Fort Sumter, was relieved with complimentary order, assigning him to higher duties, on the night of September 4th-5th. His successor was Major Stephen Elliott, and the fort became, for a time, an infantry post.

The siege of Fort Wagner had been advancing without another assault, but with the heaviest land and naval fire ever concentrated on so small a site. Against its possible, but not always efficient armament of twelve guns, the land batteries fired 24 rifle-guns and 17 mortars, while the squad-ron added 20 more of the heaviest naval guns ever used. The fire of the defense could not be as continuous as that of the attack, but it was vigorous and effective to delay the sappers. These were about completing their work and entering the ditch of Wagner, when a fruitless attack in small boats was made on Battery Gregg. It was easily re-pulsed on the night of the 5th-6th.

Finally, after a day of unprecedented fire, Fort Wagner and Battery Gregg were evacuated successfully on the night of the 6th-7th September, and their garrisons brought to Charleston. No more gallant defense had ever been made. The subjoined tabulation will prove it.

GENERAL SUMMARY FORT WAGNER.

Total number of projectiles fired against it......18,491
Estimated total tons of metal fired against it.. 1,416
Duration of siege (days)............................... 58
Total number of casualties July to September.. 318

This loss is not inclusive of that in the two assaults and in the landing on Morris Island.

Sept. 7th, 1863—Surrender of Ft. Sumter **Demanded.**

Rear Admiral Dahlgren, after demanding the surrender of Fort Sumter and being refused, engaged Fort Moultrie and the other heavy batteries of Sullivan's Island, late in the afternoon.

TYPEWRITER SUPPLIES.

Walker, Evans & Cogswell Co., 3 and 3 Broad and 117 East Bay Streets.

UMBRELLAS.

Bentschner & Visanska, 252 King Street.
J. L. David & Bro., 279, 281 King Street.

UMBRELLA MANUFACTURERS AND REPAIRERS.

J. R. Johnson & Son, 253 King Street, (Opposite Hasell.)

Sept. 8th, 1863.—Heavy Naval Attack on Ft. Moultrie.

The forts and batteries of Sullivan's Island, greatly strengthened since the 7th April, were now mounted with from seventy to eighty guns, Fort Moultrie being only one among eleven or twelve very heavy works. The inner or western division of these was the main protection of the harbor, since the silencing of Fort Sumter.

The powerful steam frigate "New Ironsides," with five monitors, engaged again the western fortifications for three hours, diverting their fire from one of the monitors aground off Cumming's Point, and on which these works of Sullivan's Island had been firing for several hours before they were engaged. This became, probably, the severest naval battle with shore-batteries fought up to date. While the grounded monitor got off that afternoon the squadron was effectually prevented from entering the harbor, or even approaching the obstructions between Sumter and Sullivan's Island. The fight was not attended with much damage or loss on either side, but the works of Sullivan's Island were never again molested after this manner.

Sept. 8th-9th, 1863—Ft. Sumter Attacked by Small Boats.

During the fight with Sullivan's Island preparations were in progress for a night attack with small boats on the ruins of Sumter. Both Gen. Gillmore and Rear-Admiral Dahlgren were arranging for the same thing. But they failed to co-operate, and only Dahlgren's boats started on the expedition. Two only out of five divisions landed at the base of the fort, and were met with so fierce a fire from the infantry of Major Elliott's garrison and the enfilading batteries of the harbor as to withdraw or surrender in twenty minutes.

The attack was made an hour after midnight, and resulted in disastrous failure; for while not a man of the garrison was hurt the naval loss was six killed, fifteen wounded and one hundred and six prisoners.

Sept. 9th-27th 1863—Nineteen Days of Quiet.

During which the Federals were fortifying the northern end of Morris Island, and the Confederates strengthening Fort Sumter.

Sept. 28th—Ft. Sumter's First Minor Bombardment.

lasting six days. Batteries of James and Sullivan's Island fire irregularly on Morris Island.

UPHOLSTERERS.

Mutual Carpet Co., 247 King Street.

WAR RELICS.

G. J. Luhn, 67 Broad Street.   Confederate Stamps, Money and Bonds, Cannon Balls, Bayonets, Canteens, Buttons, Etc., found on Morris Island.

WORSTEDS AND EMBROIDERY SILKS.

Ph. Shuckman, 255 King Street.

44

Oct 5th-6th, 1863—Attempt to blow up the "New Ironsides."

This night attack with the torpedo-boat "David," under Lieut. Glassell, of the Confederate Navy, resulted in no immediate damage to the vessel, but convinced the Admiral that the torpedo was henceforth to be considered "among certain offensive means." The brave Lieutenant and one of his men were captured, but the boat was brought back to the city by two others of the crew.

A previous attempt, with Capt. Carlin in charge of the boat, had been a failure on the night of Aug. 20th-21st, 1863.

Oct. 26th—Ft. Sumter's Second Great Bombardment.

lasting forty-one days and nights, was attended with serious loss in men and material. The total of shots fired at the fort by land and naval guns and mortars was 18,677. The casualties being 30 killed and 70 wounded. But the fort repaired nightly most of its damages, and was armed again with three heavy guns in the lower casemates opposite Fort Moultrie.

Dec. 11th, 1863—Explosion of Magazine in Fort Sumter.

This was accidental, from some cause never discovered. It was a far more serious calamity than the previous bombardment, for it was attended with fifty-two casualties, and a destructive fire, which burnt out the habitable quarters, and drove the garrison into crowded and unhealthy shelters. While the quarters were on fire, the enemy opened on the fort firing 220 rounds, which constituted the second minor bombardment. This explosion and fire marked a crisis in the fort's endurance; for, if they had been followed up with another heavy cannonade, the fort might have become untenable, at the end of a week, so reduced were the accommodations and even places of safety, and so strained and harrassed were the men of the garrison.

Jan. 29-31st, 1864—Fort Sumter's third minor Bombardment

lasting three days, with 583 rounds fired, did no more damage than could be repaired. Another Confederate armored gunboat, the "Charleston," was added to the harbor defences, after having been built in the city.

Feb. 12th, 1864—Fort Sumter mounts more Guns. making a total of six in casemates.

Feb. 17-18th. 1864—The Housatonic sunk by a Torpedo-boat.

This fine steam sloop-of-war carrying eleven guns, was sunk off Charleston bar by a "fish," or diving, torpedo-boat, attacking the sloop by night, and going to the bottom herself in the attack. Lieut. Dixon of the 21st Alabama Regiment, perished with his crew of six men. Five of the crew of the Housatonic were also drowned, the greater part escaping from the sinking vessel.

March, 1864—Fort Sumter's fourth minor Bombardment,

with firing of 143 rounds.

April 20th, 1864—Gen. Beauregard ordered to Virginia,

relieved by Major-General S. Jones.

April 28-May 4th, 1864—Fort Sumter's fifth minor Bombardment, lasting seven days, with 510 rounds.

May 4th, 1864—Lieutenant-Colonel Elliott relieved in command of Fort Sumter by Captain Mitchel.

May 13-16th, 1864—Fort Sumter's sixth minor Bombardment, lasting four days, with 1,140 rounds.

May 26th, 1864—Major-General Foster succeeds General Gillmore in command of Union troops.

May 30-June 5th, 1864—Fort Sumter's seventh minor Bombardment, lasting eight days, with 319 rounds.

July 3rd, 1864—Fort Johnson, James Island, attacked.

An expedition from Morris Island landing on the beach between Battery Simkins and Fort Johnson, nearly a thousand strong, Supports failed the charge, and 140 prisoners were taken by the Confederates, commanded by Lieutenant-Colonel Yates.

July 3-9th.—Fighting on James and John's Island.

General Foster, planning the capture of Fort Johnson in conjunction with movements by land on John's Island, and by water on Stono River, was thwarted by the Confederates in all his attempts. His intrenched position on John's Island, threatening to enfilade the James Island lines of the Confederates, was carried by their attack, and both the land and naval forces were withdrawn the next day. Union loss, 330 ; Confederate, 125, or 163.

July 7th—Fort Sumter's third great Bombardment.

lasting sixty days and nights, with a total of 14.666 rounds fired at the fort, and with 81 casualties. At first severe, the damages were soon controlled and repaired. Powder-rafts failed entirely to injure the fort. The commander, Capt. J. C. Mitchel, mortally wounded on the fourteenth day.

July 20th, 1864—The Command of Fort Sumter

passed to Capt. T. A. Huguenin, succeeding Capt. Mitchel, deceased, and continuing in command until the evacuation of the city and harbor.

GENERAL SUMMARY FORT SUMTER, FEB. 1, 1865.

Total number of projectiles fired against it...............46,053
Total weight in tons of metal thrown (estimate)......... 3,500
Total number of days under three great bombardments........ 117
Total number of days under eight minor bombardments................ 40
Total number of days under fire, steady and desultory.. 280
Total number of casualties (52 killed, 267 wounded...... 319

Jan. 15th-16th, 1865—Monitor Patapsco sunk by Torpedo

while on night picket duty between Sumter and Sullivan's Island. Before help could be given them sixty-two officers and men were carried down with the vessel, while the commander with four officers and thirty-eight men made their escape. This was the third of the armored squadron sunk off Charleston harbor, the Keokuk and the Weehawken having gone down the year before ; the latter by accidental foundering at her anchorage. The Housatonic was unarmored.

Feb. 10-12, 1865—Union demonstration on James Island,

with naval force in Stono River, and attack on rifle-pits. In consequence of the entrance into South Carolina of Gen. Sherman's army from the direction of Savannah, Georgia, the Confederates were preparing to evacuate Charleston, and only a small force was left to defend the rifle-pits in advance of the James Island lines. The enemy was held in check for four hours by these Confederate fighters of the rear-guard until one-third of the little force was either killed, wounded or captured, the commander himself being severely wounded and made prisoner. The naval fire was continued on the lines for several days and nights longer.

Feb. 12th-16th, 1865—Union demonstration on Bull's Bay,

made with land and naval forces, was resisted four days by a light battery and a small force of dismounted cavalry.

Feb. 17-18, 1865—Charleston City and Harbor Evacuated.

after 567 days of continuous military operations against them. Columbia, the capital of the State, occupied by Gen. Sherman's army.

The city of Charleston suffered little damage from the firing of the Union batteries on Morris Island. They covered with extreme range about one-half of the city, and the strain on their rifle-guns, elevated uncommonly, had the effect of bursting upwards of fifty of them. This was the fate of "The Swamp Angel," after only thirty-five discharges, and of many others that took up the firing after the evacuation of Morris Island by the Confederates in September, 1863. Heaps of rubbish here and there in the streets, and marks of conflagration, caused by explosions, were scant fruits of such great efforts. In point of military offensiveness the bombardment of Charleston was a poor substitute for not being able to get within the harbor, and capture the city. An idea of the amount of this firing may be gathered from the returns made for the winter of '63-'64, five months. In that period 2,550 shells reached the city, being at the rate of 17 *per diem*.

The city was fortified with lines on the neck, too near to be of any great value in operations from that quarter; and on its water-fronts with detached batteries generally armed with one gun only. But at White Point Garden, where the Ashley joins the Cooper River, there was a work of considerable strength, Battery Ramsay, armed with four guns, among the heaviest in the harbor.

Two others, mounted at the lower end of King Street, two at the Western end of Tradd St., (Chisolm's Mill) protected the Ashley, while two at Vanderhorst's wharf, and one at the foot of Cumberland, Laurens and Calhoun Streets, respectively, protected the Cooper River. Among the public buildings, more or less damaged by the firing, were St. Philip's and St. Michael's Churches, and the South Carolina Society's Hall in Meeting St. One of the first places struck was No. 12 Broad St., near the old Post Office, where the marks are still visible.

That our magnificent exhibit of

BLANK

BOOKS

Manufactured by us secured the

GOLD MEDAL,

GOLD MEDAL

ATLANTA 1895

proves conclusively that

WE MAKE THE VERY BEST BLANK BOOKS

made in the South.

WALKER, EVANS & COGSWELL CO.,

Charleston, S. C.